How to Handle Your TEACHER

By Roy Apps

Illustrated by Nick Sharratt

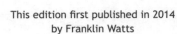

This edition first published in 2014
by Franklin Watts

Text © Roy Apps 2014
Illustrations © Nick Sharratt 2014
Cover design by Cathryn Gilbert
Layouts by Blue Paw Design

Franklin Watts
338 Euston Road
London NW1 3BH

Franklin Watts Australia
Level 17/207 Kent Street
Sydney, NSW 2000

A CIP catalogue record for this book
is available from the British Library.

(pb) ISBN: 978 1 4451 2395 0
(ebook) ISBN: 978 1 4451 2399 8
(Library ebook) ISBN: 978 1 4451 2403 2

1 3 5 7 9 10 8 6 4 2

Printed in Great Britain

Franklin Watts is a division of Hachette Children's Books,
an Hachette UK company.
www.hachette.co.uk

How to Handle Your TEACHER

By Roy Apps

Illustrated by Nick Sharratt

Contents

Introduction

Under no circumstances must you allow a
TEACHER to get hold of this book. Some
teachers can read, and if they read this
book they will get to know your teacher-
handling strategy. In other words, they will
be forewarned. And as the proverb says,
"Forewarned is forearmed." Believe me,
there's nothing more scary than a four-armed
teacher. So, there are two things you can
do to make sure your teacher doesn't read
this book...

1. You can put it somewhere your teacher will never find it — like in a block of concrete, 20 metres under the school playing field. The trouble with this solution is that you'll need a digger, a power drill and a team of navvies every time you want to read a bit of it.

2. You can flick to the "fake contents" page (see page 8) and leave the book open safely anywhere you like. If a teacher reads the book, they won't bother reading any further, because it contains things no teacher would ever have the slightest interest in.

Contents

It All Started Like This...

It was a wonderfully balmy* summer's evening. I'd just spent a couple of hours surfing the net.

And to tell you the truth, I'd finally decided that trying to fish from a surfboard was a bad idea.

I went home, logged on and checked my computer mailbox for e-mails. There weren't any.

* Dear Mr Writer, Are you sure you don't mean barmy evening? Kind regards, Adriano La Ferminnit (a.k.a. your Publisher).

So I checked my other mailbox for fe-mails, instead...

A young girl jumped out. She had a mountain bike in one hand and a large white envelope in the other.

"This is for you," she said.

"Thanks very much," I replied. "I've always wanted a mountain bike."

"Not the mountain bike!" the girl retorted. "The envelope. Read it, pea brain."

It said:

2 THAT BLOAK WOT RITES THEM HOW TERRANDLE BOOX

The girl leapt on to her saddle and pedalled off. I felt very hurt. This was because I was still holding on to the saddle at the time.

I went back inside, put my feet up on the sofa and tore open the envelope.

Inside there was a letter. In fact, there were lots of letters. And they were all written down on a page of paper like this:

Dear Bloak Wot Rites Them How Terrandle Boox,

You av dun a nace job lerning kidz ow terrandle thair mums, dads, grans, bruwversansisters and stuff. But, ime tellin yer mate, mums, dads, grans and bruwversandsisters and stuff are ded eezy terrandle kompaired to the peepole hoo make my ole heggistents sutch a flippin misserie. I meen off corse, the curse an the bane off my lyfe, TEECHERS! Theyr kompleetly an nutterly outer kontrolle! Pleez, pleez, halp a poor ole man hoosat is witzend and rite a boock lerning ev ree wun ow terrandle blooming teechers

Yours in seerly

I. Mincharge (Headteacher)

I was amazed! To think that a headteacher could write a letter like that! I mean, what is a headteacher for, if it isn't for keeping teachers under control? Goodness, some of my best friends were head teachers, not to mention some of my best fiends.

There was nothing else for it. I would have to do something I never managed to do in all my 13 years at school; I would have to do what the headteacher told me. I would have to sit down and write a book lerning ev ree wun ow terrandle blooming teechers.

BACK TO SCHOOL

To be honest, I was looking forward to writing a book called *How to Handle Your Teacher*. I thought it would be a piece of cake.* All I had to do was to refresh my memory of my days at school.

Although it was many years since I had left my school, I knew exactly where I had left it — right on the corner of Canal Street:

* I was of course, wrong. I found this out after I'd finished writing the book and then tried eating it one Sunday teatime. Yes, there was no doubt about it, *How To Handle Your Teacher* most definitely was not a piece of cake.

The first person I saw was my old teacher Mr Meesley-Grewell. He hadn't changed much, except that he wasn't so much my old teacher Mr Meesley-Grewell, more like my totally ancient teacher, Mr Meesley-Grewell.

Our conversation went something like this, or rather, it went precisely like this:

 ME: (CHEERILY) Hello, Mr Meesley-Grewell!

 MR M-G: (ANGRY) Ah, boy, have you finished it yet?

 ME: Finished what, Mr Meesley-Grewell?

 MR M-G: Your project on "Why I Think Climbing Chimneys Is An Incredibly Useful Job For a Boy To Do."

 ME: (MUTTERING) Er... my quill ran out of ink, sir.

MR M–G: I want the truth, lad!

 ME: (GOING RED AS A BEETROOT)
I haven't done it, Mr Meesley-Grewell.

 MR M–G: (FUMING) Haven't done it,
eh? You've had 35 years to finish that
piece of work!

 ME: (SHAKING FROM HEAD TO FOOT)
Yes, Mr Meesley-Grewell, sir. I know
Mr Meesley-Grewell, sir.

 MR M–G: (DEAD ANGRY) You can stay
in at break time and finish it then!

I ran away from that school just as fast
as my legs would carry me.
I fell over at the school gate
and hurt my ankle, so then
I had to run away just as
fast as I could carry my leg.

My terrifying experience with Mr Meesley-Grewell had got me thinking: 35 years ago I'd left school, but where had he been all those years? Where had all the other teachers been? Where did teachers go after school? Where did teachers come from? Or to put it another way — from come teachers did where?

I had to find out. I decided to follow Mr Meesley-Grewell home from school. Given what had happened to me when he had last seen me, I thought I'd better go under cover.

So next day at half past three, I stood outside Canal Street Primary School. And true to my word, I was under cover. Under cover of my duvet to be precise.

I followed Mr
Meesley-Grewell
along the street.
Soon he turned down
another street, then
he turned into a
large iron gate.

Amazing! I had no idea he was such a
talented magician.

Then I spotted him going up the path to a
large house. The door was open and he went
in. A brass plaque by the door read:

TEACHER CREATURES SUPPLIERS
OF GOOD QUALITY TEACHERS TO
THE NATION'S SCHOOLS
NEW OR PRE-OWNED SLIGHTLY DAMAGED
STOCK AT GREATLY REDUCED PRICES
MANAGING DIRECTOR:
PROFESSOR WATTAWALLY

I followed Mr Meesley-Grewell. Inside I found myself facing a large man wearing a gown and a mortar board.

"My name's Professor Wattawally, can I help you?" asked the man.

"I'm looking for a teacher," I said.

"New or pre-owned?" the professor asked.

"Huh?" I said.

"Bossy boots or dozy drawers?"

I shrugged.

"You obviously don't know much about teachers," said Professor Wattawally. "I suggest you sign up for my special How To Handle Your Teacher training." I signed straight away.

"Right, Mr Straight Away," said Professor Wattawally. "If you'll just follow the arrows."

"How long is the course?" I asked.

"Oh, 96 pages or so," said the professor.

"That's all right then," I said. "Only I don't want to miss netball practice."

"Get along to your first lesson, then. Follow the arrows," said Professor Wattawally.

So I did. And that is how I became an expert on how to handle teachers and was able to write this awesome book...

How To Handle Your Teacher Key Stage 1

Understanding that teachers aren't human

Now here's an interesting question: where do you come from? And I don't mean are you a Swede or a Turnip, or whether you come from Romania or Greekia. I mean, how do you come to be on planet Earth?

If you've done any PSHE at school, then of course you'll know that a stork left you under a gooseberry bush for your mum to find.

Your mum was just about to put you in the saucepan with all the gooseberries when in the nick of time she said:

"Well bless my cotton drawers! This isn't a gooseberry, it's all shrivelled. It must be a prune."

She was just going to pour a jug of custard over your head, when you went "WAAAHHH!!!" And your mum said, "Well bless my cotton drawers it's not a prune, either. It's a baby."

WAAAHHH!!

So you were brought up and taught how to clean your teeth, go to the toilet and brush your hair and then you were sent to school.

Now ask yourself this other interesting question:

where do teachers come from?

Were they dropped by storks under gooseberry bushes like the rest of us? Did they grow up to go to school like the rest of us?

The answer is — actually, I won't tell you the answer just in case there are teachers who kept reading past the trick contents on page 8. Instead I will give you a clue, but one too tricky for teachers to be able to work out.* Here's the clue:

The answer to the questions above is a two letter word that begins with:

"n" and ends with "o"

* Everyone knows teachers are hopeless at spelling.

It's obvious really. What kind of human being, if they'd been to school as a child, would then choose to spend the rest of their working lives in one? Put it another way: what kind of person in their right mind would choose to spend five days a week with the people in your class? OK, you may be an incredibly witty, intelligent and charming person — but what about some of your 29 classmates?*

* I'm thinking particularly of people like Billy Bonegrinder, Patti Poutalot, Salim Swearah, Russell Sprouts and Killer Sharkey.

Which means that your teacher must be either one or more of the following phrases. Choose one that best suits your teacher.

★ LOOPY
★ OUT OF THEIR TREE
★ A FEW GHERKINS SHORT OF A BIG MAC
★ A BLOOMING GREAT NORA
★ NOT HUMAN AT ALL

Now assuming you don't think your teachers are mad*, it stands to reason they can't be human at all.

Suddenly I jumped up in surprise. Then I jumped down again in surprise. Professor Wattawally was watching me.

"Has the penny dropped?" he asked.

"Not quite," I replied.

He let a coin fall from his hand. "It has now," he said.

---

* They will be mad if they find you've chosen any of the phrases. In fact, they'll not only be mad, they'll be livid, furious, raging, seething and wrathful as well. Not to mention just a teeny-weeny bit cross.

"Ouch!"

The penny had dropped. Right on my bad toe.

"Do you remember the brass plaque on my door?" asked Professor Wattawally.

I shook my head.

"Neither do I," said Professor Wattawally. "So let's go and see what it says again."

So we did.

TEACHER CREATURES SUPPLIERS OF GOOD QUALITY TEACHERS TO THE NATION'S SCHOOLS
NEW OR PRE-OWNED SLIGHTLY DAMAGED STOCK AT GREATLY REDUCED PRICES MANAGING DIRECTOR: PROFESSOR WATTAWALLY

"Teacher Creatures is where I make the nation's teachers," Professor Wattawally went on.

"You mean sort of Roboteachers?" I asked.

"It's not so amazing," shrugged Professor Wattawally. "After all, you get Robocops and Robochefs, so why not Roboteachers?"

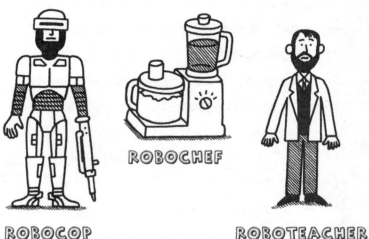

ROBOCOP

ROBOCHEF

ROBOTEACHER

A number of other facts fell into place. I made a sheet out of my duvet cover and then wrote all the facts down on it. In other words, this was my fact sheet:

FACT SHEET

FACT NUMBER ONE: Teacher Creatures was where my old teacher Mr Meesley-Grewell went every night for repairs. Being so old like a lot of teachers, his batteries were like the fizzy drinks they sell at school discos (i.e. very flat). Being old too, his belts and pulleys were getting like his jokes (i.e. wearing very thin indeed).

FACT NUMBER TWO: Mr Meesley-Grewell was an old-style Roboteacher. He had a circuit board the size of a slimming biscuit, and computer chips the size of thick-cut potato chips. When he retires from teaching, he's going to be turned into a school dinner.

FACT NUMBER THREE: I think it's about time for a quiz.

KEY STAGE 1: S.P.L.A.T.S.

(Some Pretty Looney Attempts at Testing Stuff)

Write your answers on a piece of paper.

1. How did your teacher arrive on Earth?

A: Delivered by a stork.

B: Delivered by a creamy, yellow dairy product that you spread on bread.

C: Built at Teacher Creatures.

2. Why shouldn't you let your teacher read this book?

A: Because they can't read long sentences.

B: Because they'd find it so interesting they wouldn't hear the bell and would stay in the staff room all day.

C: Because they'd find out how you are going to handle them before you do.

3. Which of the following phrases describe Roboteachers?

   A: Hard nuts.

   B: Good at chopping nuts.

   C: Going nuts.

4. Which of the following activities do Roboteachers enjoy?

   A: Beating villains up.

   B: Beating you to the front of the dinner queue.

   C: Beating eggs for a delicious cake.

5. Which of the following do Roboteachers run on?

   A: Can't run on and on without getting hopelessly out of breath.

   B: Electricity.

   C: A futuristic, self-generating power source.

ANSWERS:

Take 10 points for each correct answer:

1. A: Only people arrive this way.

   B: Can't you tell stork from butter?

   C: Is...the right answer!

2. A: Even if it is too difficult for them to read, they could still get someone else — like the school office manager — to read the long words.

   B: This is a very good reason for letting them read this book.

   C: Right! Unless you have let your teacher read this book, in which case they'll take all the points. Which is another good reason for not letting them read it!

3. A: Wrong! Robocops are this.

   B: Wrong! Robochefs do this.

   C: Right! Roboteachers always do this.

4. A: Wrong! What else does a Robocop do?

B: Correct! That's Roboteachers for you.

C: Wrong! Robochefs do this — but only when they're egged on.

5. A: Is the right answer! Roboteachers are always out of breath.

B: Wrong! Most Robochefs use electricity.

C: Wrong! Robocops run on one of these.

WHAT YOUR SCORE MEANS:

50 points: Ok smarty pants, do you want to write the rest of the book? Carry on, I don't care!

20–30 points: You're obviously trying. In fact, your teacher would probably say that you're very trying.

0–10 points: So, you think you're being taught either by an eight-foot giant clad in stainless steel armour or a food mixer. Better make an appointment with the optician. (See below.)

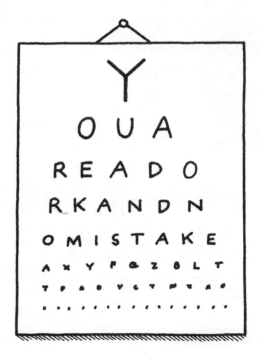

How To Handle Your Teacher Key Stage 2

Recognising and handling the most common kinds of teachers

And so it was, the following Monday morning, that Professor Wattawally sent me out on teacher-handling practice, his words of advice implanted on my brain:

"The clues to all types of teacher are to be found in the weird and wonderful clothing that they wear, all of which are specially fitted to them at Teacher Creatures." *

* And if you don't believe teachers' clothes are weird and wonderful, just take a look at what your teachers are wearing.

I stood outside a school, the name of which was strangely familiar.

But this wasn't the school I was going to visit. It was not until about nine o'clock, that I found myself outside my destination.

"There you are!" I said to myself. "I've been looking for you everywhere!"

This was a school which was so hard and tough that even the teachers walked round in pears.

And very silly they looked, too.

Then it hit me...

... I told you it was tough.

It was called the Ed Basher Academy.

"Can you tell me where the headteacher is?" I asked a girl who had a ring in her ear. When I say she had a ring in her ear, I mean she was holding a mobile phone to it. She had some mates with her and they were listening to the latest Screaming Abdabs single.

"He'll be under sedation in the medical room," said the girl. "They'll bring him back round at about four o'clock, though."

I gulped. "Under sedation? Are the pupils that difficult to handle?" I asked.

"Oh, it's not the pupils he finds difficult to handle," said the girl. "It's the teachers. Yes, we've got all types of teachers at the Ed Basher Academy."

TEACHER-TYPE 1: BOSSY BOOTS

Suddenly, we heard a voice behind us. "Suzi Woozi!" it boomed sternly to the girl. "Get yourself into school. Don't you know the bell's gone?"

"Really?" said Suzi. "Has someone stolen it?"

"Are you taking the mickey?" said the voice, which belonged to a fierce-looking teacher.*

"No, Sir," Suzi said. "I'm leaving it here."

"Get to your class," commanded the teacher. "Lessons started five seconds ago. And I'm putting your name in the late book."

"Yes, Dr Martens," said Suzi.

Dr Martens! Of course! The bootlaces as thick as liquorice sticks had been a clue, but now there was no doubt about it. With a name like Dr Martens, this had to be a BOSSY BOOTS teacher.

---

* I say the voice belonged to him, but like the bell, I suppose it might well have been stolen.

WARNING!!!

Not to be confused with GUM BOOTS teachers who are teachers who keep chewing gum down their boots.

BOSSY BOOTS TEACHER

GUM BOOTS TEACHER

"Now where is the late book?" said Dr Martens.

"Still in bed, I expect," said Suzi. "After all, it is a late book! Ha! Ha!"

"You see what I mean about the teachers being difficult to handle?" a sad-faced Suzi said to me.

"Phoo-ey!" I replied. "I've been trained in teacher handling skills by Professor Wattawally!"

So I showed Suzi Woozi how to handle BOSSY BOOTS teachers...

Handling a Bossy Boots Teacher: Tie them up in knots

Because BOSSY BOOTS teachers have most of their brains in their boots, they easily get in a muddle. The next time Dr Martens found Suzi Woozi chatting and listening to music with her mates (i.e. eight seconds later) this is what happened...

 DR MARTENS: What do you think you come to school for? To spend all morning chatting to your friends and listening to songs? Now get along to Miss Takes' room.*

---

* By which he meant Ed Basher Academy's extremely large English teacher, more commonly known as "Big" Miss Takes.

SUZI: Yessir.

 DR MARTENS: Make sure you apologise to her for your lateness.

 SUZI: Yessir.

 DR MARTENS: And see me at break.

 SUZI: Yessir.

 DR MARTENS: Well, what are you waiting for?

 SUZI: Sorry Sir, I'm trying to remember everything you said. What was the first thing?

 DR MARTENS: (HE'S FORGOTTEN) Ummm...

SUZI: Something about "What do you think you come to school for to spend...?"

 DR MARTENS: Oh yes! ...spend all morning chatting to your friends and listening to that music—

 SUZI: Can I really, sir? Oh, thank you very much, sir!

RESULT: Suzi spent all morning chatting to her mates and listening to the latest Screaming Abdabs single with Dr Martens' permission! Ye-e-eh!

Of course, there are other ways of tying a BOSSY BOOTS teacher up in knots. Probably the most effective is to use their liquorice stick bootlaces. While they are bossing one of your mates, just tie them to each other — your teacher's laces that is, not your mate to your teacher. It's tricky, but have a go. If you can master this one, then you're a natural teacher handler and should go far. Unlike your teacher.

TEACHER-TYPE 2: CLEVER CLOGS

I left Suzi Woozi with her mates and went into school. Outside the first classroom a sad-faced boy in a Man United strip approached me.

"Are you the Teacher Handler?" he asked me.

"Yes," I replied. "How did you know? Are you psychic?"

"Wow! How did you know my name?" asked Si Kick.

"Because I'm psychic too," I replied.

"Can you help us with our teacher?" said Si Kick. He led me to the classroom door. The sign read:

· MISS KNOWALL ·

Good morning, Miss Knowall.

Ah, good morning, Si.

And bonjour, buongiorno, sabah al khair, jóusàhn, guten morgen, and howdee!

Saying "good morning" in English wasn't good enough for Miss Knowall. There was no doubt about it. Miss Knowall was a CLEVER CLOGS teacher.

WARNING!!!

Not to be confused with STUPID CLOGS teachers — Roboteachers built in the 1970s who, well...just wear stupid clogs (not to mention flared trousers, tartan hats and tank tops).

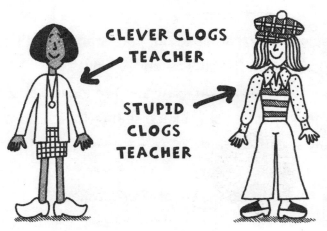

CLEVER CLOGS TEACHER

STUPID CLOGS TEACHER

"Mental arithmetic," announced Miss Knowall to the class. "What's 2678 times 758? Without using your calculators! Si?"

"12 and a half?" Si suggested.

"No!" said Miss Knowall. "Goodness, it's really a very easy sum. I see you are going to have to do extra maths homework. Now let's do some work on general knowledge. What's the name of the fantastic new star discovered by NASA?"

"Pixie Snose?" suggested Si.

"No, Si. Honestly," huffed Miss Knowall. "When I was your age I knew the name of every satellite, planet and star constellation. Now, I think we had better get to the library so you can read up about your stars — and I don't mean the silly celebrity kind!"

After the lesson I saw Si. "I've looked at so many space books, I keep seeing stars before my eyes!" he said.

I nodded.

"So how do we handle her?" asked Si.

I handed him a sheet of paper. "Everything you need to know is on here," I said.

"But the words are so small they just look like black lines," Si said. He had a good point, so I've written the words out below:

Handling a Clever Clogs Teacher: Ask a silly question

Ask any CLEVER CLOGS teacher the questions on the following pages and then watch them squirm as they try to work out the answer!

1. What is a frog's favourite drink?

Typical Clever Clogs Teacher Answer: Umm...stagnant pond water?

WRONG!!!

Right answer: Croaker Cola!

2. What do you call a dog with no legs?

Typical Clever Clogs Teacher Answer: Ummm...a noniped?

WRONG!!!

Right answer: Doesn't matter what you call him, 'cos he won't come anyway!

3. Why do bees hum?

Typical Clever Clogs Teacher Answer: Ummm...it's the sound their wings make as they vibrate the air?

WRONG!!!

Right answer: Because they don't know the words.

4. How do you make a Swiss cross?

Typical Clever Clogs Teacher Answer: Umm...you draw a vertical line and an intersecting horizontal line...

WRONG!!!

Right answer: You put ice cubes down the back of his shirt!

5. What's the proper name for a man who shears sheep?

Typical Clever Clogs Teacher Answer: Umm...a sheep shearer?

WRONG!!!

Right answer:
A Baaaaarber!

RESULT: Next lesson, I watched Miss Knowall knitting her brows. Then at last she put her needles down. "Ummm ... I don't think I do know the answer to that one, Si," she said. She spent the next hour with her head buried in every copy of *Guinness World Records* she could find in the school library. She was concentrating so hard, she didn't see Si and his classmates slip their favourite magazines inside their maths books. Ye-e-eh!

TEACHER TYPE 3: HOT SHOES

By now the word about me had spread all round the school.

"Excuse me," whispered a voice behind me. I turned round to find myself facing a lad who looked like your mum's conservatory after you've been playing football on the patio: i.e. completely shattered.

"My name's Harry Biker," said the lad. "Can you help me handle my teacher, Ms Wizbang?"

"Is something up with her?" I asked. "Something's up, down, in, out and shake it all about with her," replied Harry Biker. "You have a look through our classroom window next lesson."

So I did.

"Right class," said Ms Wizbang, "this lesson we are going to be doing RE PE PSHE and computing Ben get the pen Paul the ball Pia the gear four teams Fred you're Red Jasmeen Green Sue Blue Jack Black write on the computer about your teeth Keith the journey of the banana Rukshana underneath the story of the Ark Mark while you're running on the spot singing "Lord of the Dance" Lance yes Ness you too Hugh after three Lee..."

I was worn out just listening to Ms Wizbang. There was no doubt about it, she was a typical HOT SHOES teacher. The sort who are so full of energy, their feet never touch the ground.

WARNING!!!

Not to be confused with SNOW SHOES teachers. These are PE teachers who play tennis standing on their hands.

HOT SHOES TEACHER

SNOW SHOES TEACHER

I slipped the following note into Harry Biker's hand while he was lying on the floor exhausted at the end of the lesson.

Handling a Hot Shoes Teacher:
Just weight and wait

This method will sort out your HOT SHOES teacher in eight easy steps (quick, quick, quick, quick, slow, quick, quick, quick). Here are the steps:

1: Go to the cement shop and buy a bucket of cement.

2: Take it to school.

4: Your Hot Shoe Teacher is so panicked she leaps out of her shoes and onto her desk screaming "Eikk!"

3: When your Hot Shoes teacher arrives in class shout: "Oh look! There's a mouse under your desk, Miss!"

5: While your Hot Shoes Teacher is on her desk looking anywhere but on the floor where she thinks the nasty ickle mouse-y is, you pour the cement into her shoes.

6: You say: "It's all right, Miss. The mouse has gone. You can come down now."

7: Your Hot Shoes Teacher climbs down off her desk into her shoes which are full of cement!

8: The cement sets

RESULT: Your HOT SHOES teacher spends so much energy just trying to lift her feet up, she runs out of steam, wears herself out and falls fast asleep! This means that you and your friends can play football with the classroom globe, gossip about your fave TV shows or get stuck into reading the next page of *How to Handle Your Teacher*.

TEACHER TYPE 4: DOZY DRAWERS

I was in the reception area looking at some pictures on the wall (obviously a class project on "Monsters from the swamp" I thought, until I saw the title "Teaching Staff: Ed Basher Academy") when Anton Deck called me into his classroom. "Can you help us with our teacher, please? Her name's Miss Gonallsoppy."

I looked at the teacher sitting in front of the class. There was a faraway look in her eyes. In fact, the look was so faraway I could hardly see it.

"We can't get her to take any notice of us at all," sighed Anton Deck. "Listen to this."

I hid in the cupboard under the sink. Anton put his hand up. "Please, Miss," he said. "Leonardo, the class hamster, has escaped from his cage and is about to jump down the back of your neck."

"That's very nice, dear," beamed Miss Gonallsoppy.

"And Miss," he continued, "Ali Pally's fallen off his chair and is writhing about on the floor being consumed by a fearsome godzilla-type monster, Miss."

"Just so long as he finishes his work," said Miss Gonallsoppy, dreamily.

"You see," said Anton Deck. "She doesn't take any notice of us at all!"

"You should be grateful," I replied.

"You don't understand," said Anton. "When we do have work, it's all soppy stuff. Like learning poems which go...

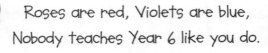

Roses are red, Violets are blue,
Nobody teaches Year 6 like you do.

and

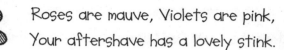

Roses are mauve, Violets are pink,
Your aftershave has a lovely stink.

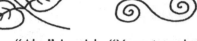

"Ah," I said. "Your teacher is a classic example of a DOZY DRAWERS type teacher."

WARNING!!!

Not to be confused with CHEST OF DRAWERS teachers.

CHEST OF DRAWERS TEACHER

DOZY DRAWERS TEACHER

"DOZY DRAWERS teachers are usually in lurv with another teacher in the school," I explained.

Anton nodded. "It's Mr Hunk, the new student teacher." He sighed. "What can I do? Even when I do really good work, like my story about the Mutant Tomato Which Ate Babies, she still puts lots of crosses on it."

"That's because she's practising writing kisses," I explained.

"And another thing," said Anton. "She's threatened to get us all to make soppy Valentine cards in art."

"What you need," I told him, "is one of these…"

Handling a Dozy Drawers Teacher: The all-purpose lurv-letter

Cross out any inappropriate words, sign with the name of the teacher your teacher is in lurv with and leave it on your teacher's desk:

Sweetikins*

My darlingest sweatikins**

Swotikins***

I think about you all the time. Your hair has the scent of flowers/cauliflowers. Your cheeks are like peaches/football peaches. Your eyes are like saucers/flying saucers. Your lips are like petals/bicycle petals.

Your ever loving honey pie

...(teacher's name)

* I know it's amazing, but this is how teachers who are in lurv talk to each other.

** I know it's amazing, but this is how PE teachers who are in lurv talk to each other.

*** I know it's amazing, but this is how student teachers who are in lurv talk to each other.

RESULT: When Anton Deck put a copy of this on Miss Gonallsoppy's desk, she was out of lurv with Mr Hunk before you could say "lovey-dovey". Anton and his mates didn't have to make Valentine's cards in art. In fact,

they made paper whizzo-bombers, just like
they always did in the good days before Miss
Gonallsoppy was in lurv.

TEACHER TYPE 5:
WOOLLY HAT

I sauntered out into the playground. A group
of boys was playing football. They had already
broken every downstairs classroom window.
Now I knew why they called it break time.

I was hiding behind the dustbins making a few notes — mainly £10 and £20 ones — when Ali Pally came up to me.

"Can you tell me how to handle my teacher, please?" he asked.

"What's wrong with her?" I replied.

"That's what's wrong with her," said Ali Pally. He pointed to the teacher on playground duty.

Even though it was a warm, sunny day, she was wearing a woolly hat. She was skipping around singing, "In and out the dusty bluebells; who will be my master." I couldn't imagine anyone being her master, not even Master Obi Wan Kenobi.

"Give us a break, Miss Craysey," said Ali. CRASH! went another classroom window. It wasn't Miss Craysey giving him or anyone else a break, it was the lads playing football. Miss Craysey was too busy singing "In and out the dusty bluebells" to have noticed them.

"Your Miss Craysey is a classic example of a WOOLLY HAT teacher," I said. "Or to put it more correctly, a WALLY HAT teacher."

WARNING!!!

Not to be confused with WELLY HAT teachers. These are simply teachers who like walking in the school pond — on their heads.

"Can she be cured?" asked Ali.

WALLY HAT TEACHER

WELLY HAT TEACHER

"If she's a side of bacon, she can," I replied.

"Help!" said Ali.

Miss Craysey was coming over. "Ali!" she called. "You can come and dance 'In and Out the Dusty Bluebells' with me."

"Sorry Miss, I've badly hurt my ankle," mumbled Ali.

"Nonsense!" yelled Miss Craysey as she hauled him off into the playground, where much to the merriment of all his friends, she whirled him in and out the dusty bluebells.

I observed proceedings from behind the dustbins. It was painful to watch. Mainly because the caretaker came out and threw

14 sacks of rubbish on my head.

Later on, in the medical bay, while I was having my head bandaged up and Ali was being treated for shock, I was able to go through with him the principal points of handling a WALLY HAT teacher, and here they are...

Handling a Woolly Hat Teacher: Act daft

The only way to handle a WOOLLY or WALLY HAT teacher is to act as daft as they are.

So when Ali was asked to dance with Miss Craysey, instead of saying he'd hurt his ankle, which was a very sensible answer, he should've said something completely daft, like "Sorry Miss, I'm allergic to gherkins," leaving her too bewildered to make him do anything.

Here are some typical WALLY HAT teacher requests, with some pretty useless sensible replies and some really useful daft replies:

Typical Wally Hat Teacher Requests	Sensible Replies	Useful Daft Replies
Let's all pretend we're trees!	Can I do extra maths instead? RESULT: You have to do extra maths.	Please Miss, I've just turned into a chain-saw. RESULT: You spend the lesson going nee-ahhh!!
Where is your homework?	Sorry Miss, I forgot it. RESULT: Kept in at break.	Please Miss, we've got an alien staying with us and he ate it. RESULT: Your WOOLLY HAT teacher gives you a packet of biscuits for your alien's tea.

Jammie *Dodgers*

Typical Wally Hat Teacher Requests	Sensible Replies	Useful Daft Replies
Who's going to help me make a giant pansy out of cardboard tubes? 	Sorry Miss, I'm no good with my hands RESULT: You get to be the giant pansy instead.	Excuse me Miss, the Draj of Zogma calls me from beyond the stars. RESULT: You get the afternoon off as the inter-galactic space bus leaves at five past two.
Where is your homework?	Sorry Miss, I forgot it. RESULT: Kept in at lunch time.	Please Miss, it turned into a packet of cereal. RESULT: You have to bring a packet of cornflakes the next day.

Typical Wally Hat Teacher Requests	Sensible Replies	Useful Daft Replies
Who'd like to sponsor me in the School Fête Goat-Yoghurt-Eating competition?	Sorry Miss, I haven't got any any money. RESULT: You have to take part in the competition as well.	Sorry Miss, I'm a fruitarian. RESULT: Your teacher sends you home to get better.
Where is your homework?	Sorry Miss, I forgot it. RESULT: Kept in at afternoon break.	Please Miss, Tom Daley stole it on the way to school. RESULT: You're given the day off to go diving after him.

KEY STAGE 2: S.P.L.A.T.S.
(Some Pretty Looney Attempts at Testing Stuff)

Test your knowledge of different types of Roboteacher:

1. On a piece of paper match the following Roboteachers with the equipment needed to be able to handle them properly:

TYPE OF TEACHER HANDLING

   a) Woolly Hat   **d)** Clever Clogs

   b) Dozy Drawers   **e)** Hot Shoes

   c) Bossy Boots

EQUIPMENT NEEDED

   (i) Cement

   (ii) Liquorice stick bootlaces

   (iii) Lurv letter

   (iv) An exercise-book-eating alien

   (v) A copy of *One Hundred And One Silly Questions to Make Your Teacher Squirm*

SCORE: 10 points for each correct answer.

WHAT YOUR SCORE MEANS:

40–50 points: You've got the makings of a CLEVER CLOGS teacher.

30–40 points: You've got the brains of an exercise-book-eating alien.

20–30 points: You've got the brains of a liquorice stick.

10–20 points: You've got the brains of a teacher.

0–10 points: You've got the brains of two teachers.

How To Handle Your Teacher Key Stage 3

Amazing! New! Improved! Teachers and how to recognise them

As you've probably realised, all the types of teacher we've looked at so far have been really old. However, the Teacher Creature factory has been busy developing amazing, new and improved types of teacher.

I was invited to take a look at some of these state-of-the-art teachers. Some had taken up posts in the country's toppermost schools:

Others had taken up posts in some of the country's bottommost schools:

This didn't please the games teachers.

I had a choice of schools to visit. One was the country's top public school. I got there for lunch, but then I found it was Eton.

In the end I decided to visit a little place called Downwith School. Here I found five examples of the most modern and up-to-date teachers ever invented:

1: THE JOGGERAPHY TEACHER

No sooner had I walked through the school gates than I saw a crowd of children jogging round the playground each of them dressed in a different national costume. At their head was a teacher wearing not a whistle, but a compass round his neck. There was no doubt about it. This was the new model Roboteacher Mr Charles Atlas, a special money-saving combined PE and geography teacher, known as a joggeraphy teacher.

I left Mr Atlas just as he was about to kick off a game of football — using a globe instead of a ball, of course.

2: THE HOLOGRAM TEACHER

Next I walked straight through the school hall, straight through the adjoining classroom and straight through the teacher who was standing there.

"**Aaaargh!!!!**"

Then I said, "Hello!"

"Hollo!" said the teacher.

"Yes, you are, aren't you," I replied. "Completely hollow."

"How could this be?" I asked myself.

"How should I know?" replied myself.

Then I saw the name plate on her door:

· MISS ELSE WARE ·

...it said. Amazing, I thought: a name plate that can talk!

It explained everything though. The reason the teacher was completely hollow and I had been able to walk right through her was obvious: she was elsewhere! In other words, she was a hologram teacher. She wasn't really there. She was really in the staff room drinking mugs of coffee. It was just her hologram which I could see in the classroom.

Now, as you can imagine, just about every teacher in the world wants to be a hologram, so they can sit in the staff room all day,

except for these two who
are really not really
there.

Miss Ing Brain: who
teaches recorder part-
time. She's a teacher
who isn't really all
there. Not even on Monday and Wednesday
afternoons when she is, if you
see what I mean.

Mr Potts: who
teaches art and is out
of this world.

Being a hologram is also dead useful in lots
of other ways. For example, when
you try the usual harmless
everyday tricks on your
teacher, like putting a live
frog in her handbag...

Ribbit

...or putting a bucket of iced water above the door for when they come in...

...or connecting the "Extra Homework" book to a two zillion volt electricity supply, it doesn't have any effect on them whatsoever.

If you want to check whether or not your teacher is a hologram, you can conduct this really simple experiment:

THE IS-MY-TEACHER-A-HOLOGRAM?-TEST

FIRST STEP: Walk through her. Or him. If you come out the other side, then your teacher is a hologram. If you fall flat on your bottom on the floor, your teacher is not a hologram.

In fact, they are more likely to be a hollergram.

3: THE HOLLERGRAM TEACHER

Creating a hologram teacher is, of course, a tricky business. Things do go wrong. So much so that I heard there were three mutant forms of hologram teacher at Downwith School. And when I say heard, I mean heard—

Yelled a voice loud enough to have woken a hibernating warthog.

"Ah," I said. "Fancy bumping into you!"

Actually that wasn't exactly true, in fact it wasn't even inexactly true. I've never fancied bumping into any kind of teacher and this one was one of the least bumpable-into teachers I'd ever come across. The thing was, I'd bumped into this teacher, having mistaken him for a hologram. I knew he was a hollergram teacher and not a hologram teacher as soon as I heard him speak. Like all hollergram teachers he hollered with lots and lots of exclamation marks. He had black rimmed glasses, a funny moustache and a cigar. There was no doubt about it, he was Mr Groucho Marx, one of the Exclamation Marx brothers.

YOU!!!!!! YOU SILLY PERSON!!!!

hollered Mr Marx. (Told you he was a groucho.)

ME: (meekly) Me, sir?

MR MARX: YES, YOU SIR!!!!! WHAT DID YOU WALK INTO ME LIKE THAT FOR?

ME: Sorry, sir.

MR MARX: YOU COULD HAVE DONE SOME

SERIOUS DAMAGE!!!* DIDN'T YOU SEE ME?

ME: Sorry, sir. I thought you were a hooligan
er... I mean a hologram, sir.

MR MARX: GRRR!!!

ME: Have you got anything else to shout...er,
I mean say, sir, or shall I just crawl into
this hole**?

4: THE HORROR-GRAM TEACHER

I was just having my lunch at Downwith School
when I saw Mr Alucard. I wished I hadn't. Mr
Alucard is a horror-gram teacher. Horror-gram
teachers make Lord Voldemort look like Mary
Poppins. Mr Alucard, the horror-gram teacher
at Downwith School looked like this***:

* He's right. Hollergram teachers are usually so big that if
they fall over they end up doing some serious damage...
** The hole the hollergram teacher made when I knocked him
over, that is.
*** WARNING: Readers of a nervous disposition, or even
a nervous indisposition should skip over the next picture by
carefully placing this book on the floor,
then getting a rope and simply
skipping over it.

I tried to get rid of Mr Alucard by driving a steak through his heart. Unfortunately, the steak I was eating for my school lunch turned out to be a soya-bean rissole,

so Mr Alucard didn't wither away into a sticky mass of goo before my very eyes, or vanish in a cloud of ash. In fact, the only sticky mass of goo before my very eyes was my jam pudding and custard for afters.

5: THE SUPER ROBOT TEACHER

Finally, I came across a super robot teacher at Downwith School called Mr Triffick. Wow!

Awesome! Cool! I can hear you thinking.*

You're imagining a super teacher, aren't you? The sort who gives you two-hour break times, forgets about spulling tasts,** sets your homework as watching 20 episodes of *Teenage Mutant Ninja Turtles* and makes Barry Bludgeon*** stand upside-down with his face in the recycling bin for two hours. Forget it! — not the spulling tasts! I mean Mr Triffick was a Super Robot Teacher. The sign on his door said:

```
NEW FROM TEACHER
CREATURES SUPER ROBOT
TEACHER MR TRIFFICK BA
LOTS OF GIGABYTES!!!
AMAZING RAM!!!
```

---

* You really should get your brain oiled, you know.
** Dear Mr Writer, Do you mean spilling tosts? Kind regards, Adriano La Ferminnit (a.k.a. your Publisher).
*** The class bully.

Yes, Mr Triffick was a Teacher With Improved Technology — or TWIT for short. His RAM was really amazing. Well, have you ever seen a pet sheep that can hum the theme tune to *Doctor Who*?

Ba baa! Ba baaaa! Ba ba ba...

Mr Triffick did have lots of GIGABYTES, too. Unfortunately, these were on his leg where his amazing RAM had sunk his teeth into his shin. In many ways, Mr Triffick looked like his pet RAM, too. Hardly surprising really: he was a BA after all.

"Right," said Mr Triffick, "there are just four words for your spalling tist tomorrow. They are 'Turtles', 'Ninja', 'Mutant', 'Teenage'. Your maths homework is to work out exactly how many words there are in your spalling tist."

I did say he was a TWIT. It looked as if this teacher with improved technology could do with his technology being upgraded even further.

Just then Mr Alucard came along. He had his eye on Mr Triffick's RAM. It looked at first as if he was for the chop. Then it looked as if he was the chop*.

I turned on my heel and ran out of Downwith School.

I turned the corner and ran out of breath. Then I turned another corner and ran out of... paper.

* The mutton chop Mr Alucard was planning for his dinner, that is.

KEY STAGE 3: S.P.L.A.T.S.
(Some Pretty Looney Attempts at Testing Stuff)

1. What do you call a teacher who wears a compass instead of a whistle around their neck?

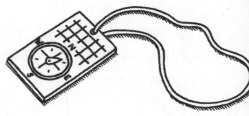

A: Lost.

B: A complete numpty.

C: A joggeraphy teacher.

2. Which of the following three things is the most dangerous and terrifying to walk into?

A: A plate glass door.

B: A graveyard at midnight.

C: A hologram teacher.

3. Which of the following makes the most hideous racket?

A: The lead singer of the Screaming Abdabs.
B: A herd of elephants with stomach ache.
C: A hollergram teacher.

4. Which of the following three hideous monsters is likely to give you nightmares?

A: A headless corpse.
B: Godzilla's granny.
C: A horror-gram teacher.

5. What do the letters TWIT stand for?

A: Teacher With Impressive Tattoo.
B: Teacher With Ink-stained Tie.
C: Teacher With Improved Technology.

SCORE: All right answers 1,000 points.

WHAT YOUR SCORE MEANS:

6,000–8,000 points:

Congratulations! You've reached Level 4. Now when you've finished, come back down again.

4,000–6,000 points:

Pathetic! Now get down to the graveyard at midnight and see if you can answer the Spanish Inquisition's questions, you complete wazzock. And take Godzilla's granny with you!

0–4,000 points:

Appalling! Go back to school. Nursery school, that is. And take that headless corpse with you, but don't let them frighten the little kiddies!

How To Handle Your Teacher Key Stage 4

Learning about just what goes on in the staff room

We all know what happens to teachers at break time and lunch time: they race off to the staff room and lock themselves in until the bell goes again. But what do they get up to when they're in there?

Let's open the staff room door at Ed Basher Academy and have a look...

Of course! In their staff room, teachers do everything they've told you not to do in the classroom.

prattle prattle

gossip gossip

They put their feet up on the furniture.

natter natter

They pick their noses.

drone drone

gab gab

They eat.

They sniff their armpits.

chat

chat

burble burble

They ping bits of paper at Mr E B Jeebies.

They talk. And talk. And talk. And talk.

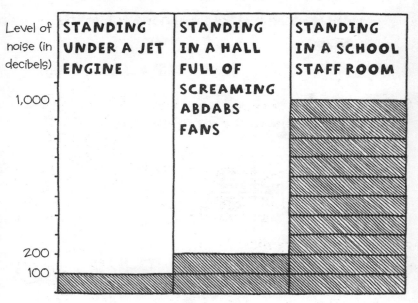

Level of noise (in decibels)

| STANDING UNDER A JET ENGINE | STANDING IN A HALL FULL OF SCREAMING ABDABS FANS | STANDING IN A SCHOOL STAFF ROOM |

1,000

200
100

The next thing the teachers do is to all go "lp Dip Sky Blue Who's It Not You". Then who ever is "it", has to go out on playground duty. That's Miss Gonallsoppy.

Next, those who are left recharge their batteries. And I don't mean they plug themselves into the power socket, though given the fact that teachers are robots, they might just as well.

Typical goings-on in a Roboteacher's staff room

TEACHERS' DIET:

★ High optic fibre.

★ Electrical juice.

★ Micro chips.

STOKING THE FIRE:

★ Really ancient teachers who are steam-powered run on coke and water.

FRYING CHIPS:

★ What Roboteachers do when they've blown a fuse.

How To Handle Your Teacher Key Stage 5

Learning about the power source

TURN HERE

To really understand how Roboteachers work you have to understand their power source. This is the power source in a typical school:

HEADTEACHER
Runs into his/her office.

DEPUTY HEADTEACHER
Runs a shower (after taking Year 5 for PE).

SCHOOL OFFICE MANAGER
Runs the Headteacher.

PARENT
Runs you to school and back in the car.

SCHOOL HAMSTER
Runs round and round getting nowhere.

SCHOOL GOVERNOR
Runs round and round getting nowhere.

THE SCHOOL CLEANERS

Run mops round the school. These people are so dangerous they're only allowed in after school's finished.

THE DINNER LADIES

Run the lunch box trolleys over your feet. These formidable people used to serve Batman his lunch. ("Dinner, dinner, dinner, dinner Batman!!!" they used to sing.)

THE SCHOOL SITE MANAGER!!!!
(a.k.a. the Scaretaker) Runs the school.

There! I had finished it! Just like Mr I
Mincharge, the headteacher had asked me to.

One last problem remained. How to get the
manuscript of *How To Handle Your Teacher*
to the publishers safely without any nosey
teachers getting hold of it!

Then I remembered my very first thought
on starting to write the book. I thought *How
to Handle Your Teacher*
would be a piece of
cake. Quickly I
put this piece
of paper over
the book:

Now *How To Handle Your Teacher* really was
a piece of cake.

"Ah ha," said a voice behind me. It was Dr
Martens, the BOSSY BOOTS teacher. "What
are we trying to hide in there?"

"Nothing, Sir," I said.

"Nothing?" said Dr Martens. "That doesn't look like nothing. What is it? Let's have the truth. I wasn't born yesterday. What do you think I am?"

"A fruit-cake, Sir," I said.

Dr Martens was beginning to look like a sauna, in other words very steamed up. I raced out of Downwith School and ran all the way to my publisher's office in Deadline Lane.

And the rest, as they say, is history. Not to mention geography, English, maths, science, PSHE, art, computing, PE, games...

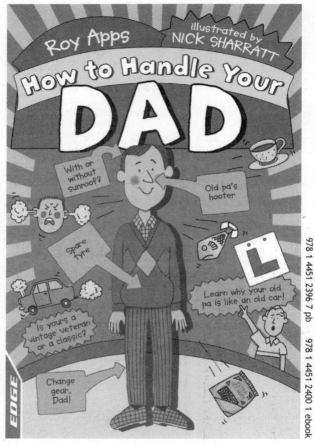

Dads can be a heap of trouble.
Dads can be a fashion car crash
...but Dads keep chugging along.

Like most dads, yours probably has bits falling off and finds it hard to get started in the morning. And like most kids, you probably think you'll never get more pocket money out of him...

How to Handle Your Dad is here to "help" with all your dad-related breakdowns. Even your dad can be transformed into a top-of-the-range model!